How can I deal with...

Bullying

D1364470

Sally Hewitt

W
FRANKLIN WATTS
LONDON • SYDNEY

This edition 2011

Franklin Watts
338 Euston Road
London NW1 3BH

Franklin Watts Australia
Level 17/207 Kent Street
Sydney, NSW 2000

Series editor: Sarah Peutrill
Art director: Jonathan Hair
Design: Susi Martin
Picture researcher: Diana Morris
Series advisor: Sharon Lunney

A CIP catalogue record for this book is
available from the British Library.

Dewey number: 362.7
ISBN: 978 1 4451 0624 3
Printed in China

Franklin Watts is a division of Hachette
Children's Books, an Hachette UK company.
www.hachette.co.uk

Picture credits:
John Birdsall/John Birdsall
Photography: front cover main, 7, 18.
Sean Cayton/Image Works/Topfoto: 14.
Bob Daemmrich/Imageworks/Topfoto:
26. fotovisage/Alamy : 13. Tony
Freeman/Art Directors: 9. Spencer
Grant/Art Directors: 21. Jeff
Greenberg/Art Directors: 4. Jeff
Greenberg/ImageWorks/Topfoto: 28
Henry King/Photonia/Getty Images: 8.
R J Livermore/Art Directors: 25.
Brian Mitchell/Photofusion: 5, 19.
David Montford/Photofusion: 6.
Helene Rogers/Art Directors: 12, 24
Ellen Senisi/Image Works/Topfoto : 10,
11. 22. Bob Turner/Art Directors: 15.
Libby Welch/Photofusion: 27.

What can Winnie do?

She can:

✔ tell her friends that she doesn't like bullying

✔ make new friends if the children in the gang still want to be bullies

✔ tell her teacher what is happening.

What Winnie did

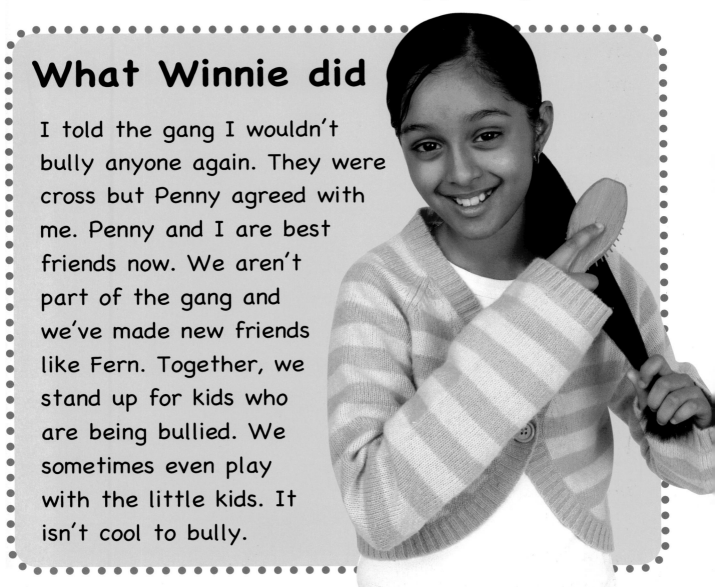

I told the gang I wouldn't bully anyone again. They were cross but Penny agreed with me. Penny and I are best friends now. We aren't part of the gang and we've made new friends like Fern. Together, we stand up for kids who are being bullied. We sometimes even play with the little kids. It isn't cool to bully.

Gus's story

My friends kept picking on a little kid in the playground. They said they were just teasing him. But when he got upset and cried, they didn't stop. At first I didn't do anything, but I felt bad. Even though I didn't join in, I felt as if I had been bullying him too.

In the end, I told my friends to leave the little kid alone. I took him to the teacher on duty. My friends stopped picking on him after that.

They make fun of my unch!

Jade's story

My mum cooks everything for my lunch box. She won't give me food and drink in packets and cartons like everyone else has. Every day, some kids grab my lunch box. They open it and say, "What rubbish has Jade's mum made for her today?"

They drop my lunch on the floor. Sometimes they throw it away.

I'm always hungry and I'm getting skinny!

I hate it when people are rude about my mum. I wish she would give me the same food as everyone else, but she says it's not good for me. I haven't told her what the kids do to my lunch!

Shelly's story

I like doing good work at school. I put my hand up first and get the answers right.

I get lots of smiley stickers and gold stars.

But some kids in my class started calling me, "Teacher's pet!"

They hid my books. They threw my school bag in the bin. They said they'd beat me up if I told anyone. Now I don't work hard or put my hand up anymore.

They laugh at me when I get into trouble – which is all the time!

What can Shelly do?

Giving in to the bullies isn't making Shelly happy.
She can:

✔ remember, there's nothing wrong with working hard and doing well
✔ tell her friend Aisha why she is getting bad marks
✔ tell her parents and her teacher.

What Shelly did

I told Mum and Dad about the bullies. They talked to my teacher. They all said I should be proud of doing well.

So I started working hard, but the bullies were worse than before!

So I told my teacher – again.

I don't know what she did, but the bullies suddenly stopped bullying me. I'm glad they didn't win.

Marcus's story

Tommy aged 8 months

I was the only child for a long time. Then Tommy arrived. Mum and Dad gave him all the love and attention. I wished Tommy had never been born and we could go back to the way we were before. I didn't realise I was bullying Tommy until Nat made me think. I don't like bullies!

Anyway, I suppose it's not Tommy's fault. Now I'm trying to be nicer to Tommy, he isn't quite so annoying!

How to get help if you are being bullied

If you are being bullied, you can feel very lonely. If you talk to someone, they can help you. You could talk to your mum or dad or another grown up in your family, your brother or sister or a friend.

Your school will have a policy on what to do about bullying, so you could talk to your teacher.

You may think that telling someone will only make things worse. If so, you can:
✔ ring Childline
✔ visit websites (see page 29).

Remember, bullying is always wrong. You don't have to put up with it.

Glossary

Bullying
Bullying is when someone hurts you or makes you unhappy and afraid on purpose.

Gang
A gang is a group of friends who go round together and play together.

Giving in
You give in to someone when they make you do something you don't want to do.

Lonely
You can feel lonely when you don't have many friends and spend a lot of time on your own.

Policy
A policy is a set of ideas and rules. A school bullying policy sets out what should be done if anyone is being bullied at school.

Popular
Someone is popular when people like them and they have a lot of friends.

Proud
You feel proud when you are pleased with something you have done and are happy for other people to know about it.

Secret
When you have a secret, you keep something to yourself and don't tell anyone about it.

Share
You share when you tell or give things to other people and you don't keep things to yourself.

Unkind
You are unkind when you do or say something that makes someone else unhappy.

Further information

For children
www.childline.org.uk
Tel: 0800 1111
Childline is the free helpline for children in the UK.
You can talk to someone about any problem and they will help you to sort it out.

http://kidshealth.org/kid/
feeling/emotion/bullies.html
Learn about bullies and how to deal with them.

In Australia
www.kidshelp.com.au
Tel: 1800 55 1800
Kidshelp is the free helpline for children in Australia. You can talk to someone about any problem.

Note to parents and teachers: Every effort has been made by the Publishers to ensure that these websites are suitable for children, that they are of the highest educational value, and that they contain no inappropriate or offensive material. However, because of the nature of the Internet, it is impossible to guarantee that the contents of these sites will not be altered. We strongly advise that Internet access is supervised by a responsible adult.

For parents
www.besomeonetotell.org.uk
Helpline for parents:
0808 800 2222
Parentline Plus offers advice, guidance and support for parents who are concerned about bullying in their child's life, both outside and within school.

www.kidscape.org.uk
A website helping to prevent bullying.

BBC health
www.bbc.co.uk/health/
physical_health/
child_development/
teen_bully.shtml

www.direct.gov.uk/en/
Parents/index.htm
Government advice for parents. In 'Common parental concerns' under 'Your child's health and safety' there is advice on bullying.

Index

Notes for parents, carers and teachers

When children are bullied, they need the support of adults to help them deal with it. But they are often reluctant to talk about it. Depression, low self-esteem and poor results at school can be signs that they are being bullied.

• Adults can look out for signs that a child is being bullied.
• Children need to know that being bullied is not their fault.
• Bullying should always be taken seriously.
• Fear of making things worse can stop children telling anyone. They need to know that it's best to tell an adult, who will take effective action where necessary.

Page 4 Maria's story
Maria is feeling lonely and left out of her group of friends at school.
• Knowing what makes a friend a good friend can help children to choose their friends well and to be a good friend to other children.

Page 9 Kurt's story
Kurt is unhappy because the children at his new school laugh at him for being different.
• Understanding that being different is not wrong can help children to appreciate other people and to build their own self-confidence.

Page 12 Tamsin's story
Tamsin is frightened to go out to play at school because bigger children are bullying her.
• Children need effective intervention from an adult if they are being bullied by bigger children.

Page 15 Winnie's story
Winnie's friends are bullies. She knows it's wrong to join in but doesn't know how to stop.
• Adults can make it clear that bullying is unacceptable and never cool, and support a child who wants to stop bullying.

Page 19 Jade's story
Jade is being bullied because she brings healthy food to school for lunch.
• Being different, for example by eating healthy food, is not wrong. An adult can help tackle the bullies and protect the child who is different.

Page 22 Shelly's story
Shelly is deliberately doing badly at school so that other children don't call her 'teacher's pet'.
• It's hard for to stand up to bullies on their own. An adult can support children and help them not to give in to bullies.

Page 25 Nat's story
Marcus doesn't realise he is bullying his little brother.
• Children can be bullies without meaning to be. An adult can point out what they are doing and help them to change their behaviour.

Page 28 Playscript, Vick and Bertie's story
Children could 'perform' the parts in this simple playscript and then discuss what happened to each character, including possible reasons why Vick was a bully and what it did to his friendships.